this body
mystery

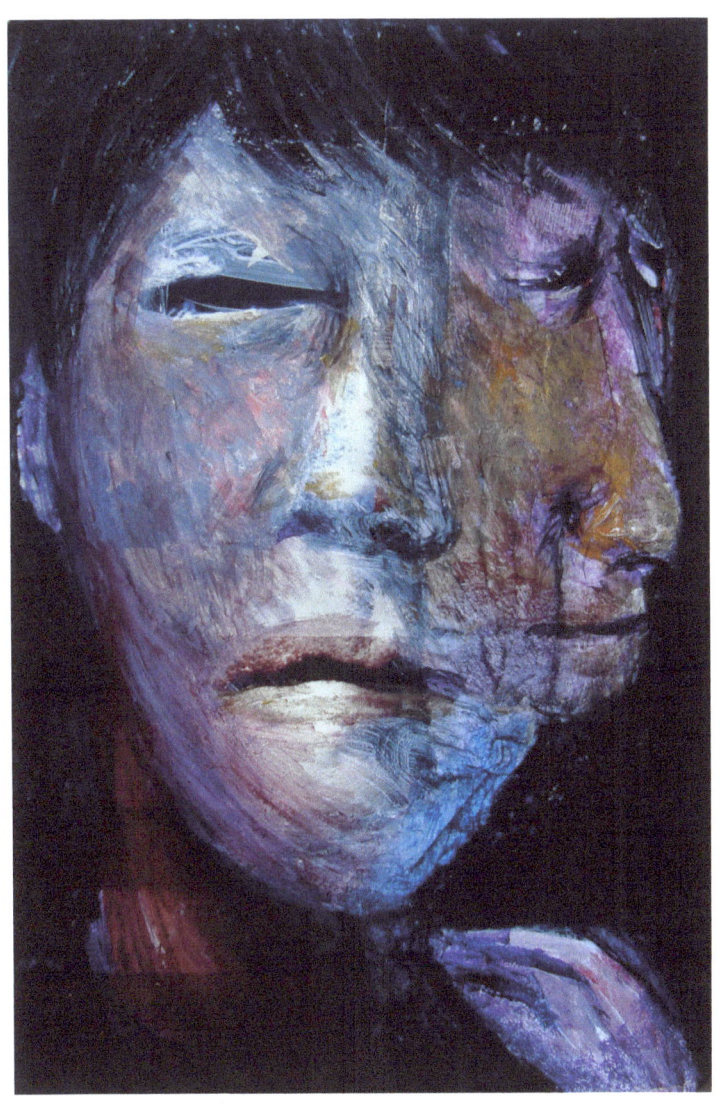

this body mystery

PAINTINGS
and POEMS | by Chath pierSath

ABINGDON SQUARE PUBLISHING
New York

This Body Mystery
is published by
Abingdon Square Publishing, Ltd.
463 West Street, Suite G122
New York, NY 10014 USA
www.abingdonsquarepublishing.com

ISBN 978-0-9830762-0-9
Library of Congress Control Number: 2012932357

First Printing: February 2012
Printed in the United States of America

Book Design: Abingdon Square Publishing

Cover Art: *This Body Mystery* © 2011 Chath pierSath
All Artwork © 2011 Chath pierSath

Acknowledgements
*I would like to thank Doug Baulos for helping me with the poems
and Massaru Goto and Yumi for their work
to raise awareness about HIV/AIDS in Cambodia.*
— *Chath pierSath*

After, a book of poems by Chath pierSath,
is also available from Abingdon Square Publishing

PREFACE

If there is anything at all that we can learn from life is that death is an integral part of it. We breathe death into our lungs, and our body is only an ephemeral shell, a borrowed existence we all shall pay in our death. Cambodia is a Buddhist country where her people look to faith to overcome their losses, sorrow and disappointments. Karma is part of people's everyday consciousness, whether one will turn out good or bad in the next life is determined by what one does in this life. I, however, don't share this belief in karma or fate or destiny. I don't believe in heaven or hell in the afterlife. I just know that good or bad karma will create heaven or hell for you here on earth. What you do to others, others will do to you. It is very universal because every faith in the world teaches this. I don't, however, believe that people I have written for in this book, deserve this sort of bad karma of prolonged suffering and pain, though they themselves thought that what they had was the result of what they did in the last life. HIV/AIDS is still a Pandemic and because we're humans, our drive to love and connect physically had resulted in great losses and sorrows.

The countless lives lost to AIDS globally tremendous and emotionally and physically exhausting, and we are still fighting AIDS. It's not over. The cure is still not here. It is only through education and self-awareness that we can prevent this form of transmission from one person to the next. Because this is a human behavior, it is difficult to curb especially in places where access to information is hard to come by and illiteracy rate is high.

This Body Mystery represents some of the Cambodian voices that have died of AIDS. I dedicate the work to them.

— *Chath pierSath*

INTRODUCTION

I first went to Cambodia in 1992. That time the Khmer Rouge and the Phnom Penh government were still fighting in the north. I was working on a photo documentary about the continued conflicts in Battambang during the time. I noticed that this one local hospital was full of patients after heavy clashes. After the civil war had ended, however, I went back to the same hospital and saw that it was still full of patients. This time, most of the patients were infected with HIV. They were dying left and right from AIDS. It was as if I had entered the very same hospital with all these wounded and sick people. This time, the physical and psychological wounds were ones of prolonged suffering, despair and hopelessness.

I started to take photographs of them in 1999, which forced me to want to do more for the people, as my relationship with them deepened. I saw that there was no adequate care, no medicines and there was one doctor for all of them. Some of the patients had no family. They were often rejected from their community, and they were left abandoned to die. I decided to start an international awareness campaign to bring needed attention in support of these patients in the hospital, but also to raise a general awareness that throughout Cambodia, AIDS was beginning a new killing field. This was when I met Chath pierSath, while I was campaigning and I saw his poems and paintings. His poems deeply impressed me so I had asked him to join me in the fight against HIV/AIDS. I shared with him my photographs of the HIV/AIDS patients and this inspired him to write the poems that are in this compilation. In their voices, he managed to capture the human suffering and the loneliness, maybe the thinking and feeling behind the individuals I photographed. His poems, which are written in the voices of those who would not otherwise able to express for themselves and my photographs depicting their day to day struggle for survival, can, indeed, serve as powerful medians, in which others can sympathize in their common humanity and the suffering which we all shared. My photographs, along with Chath's poems, were exhibited in Bangkok during the International AIDS Conference in 2004, and Tokyo after, traveling around the world.

Chath left Cambodia at the age of 10 in 1979, during which, there was still heavy fighting between the Vietnamese backed government and the Khmer Rouge. He returned to Cambodia in 1994 after UNTAC monitored democratic elections to work as a volunteer. Coincidentally, he happened to be working on HIV/AIDS awareness campaign and human rights. Although the HIV infection rate has now been contained and lowered due to aggressive educational campaign, and those infected can now access medications that they can afford, Chath continues to bring awareness of the suffering of others through his writing. This book of poems contributes to the needed understanding of how AIDS can destroy many lives and break apart communities, and leave many children orphaned.

— *Masaru Goto/Photographer*

CONTENTS

OTHER POEMS

this body
          mystery

paintings

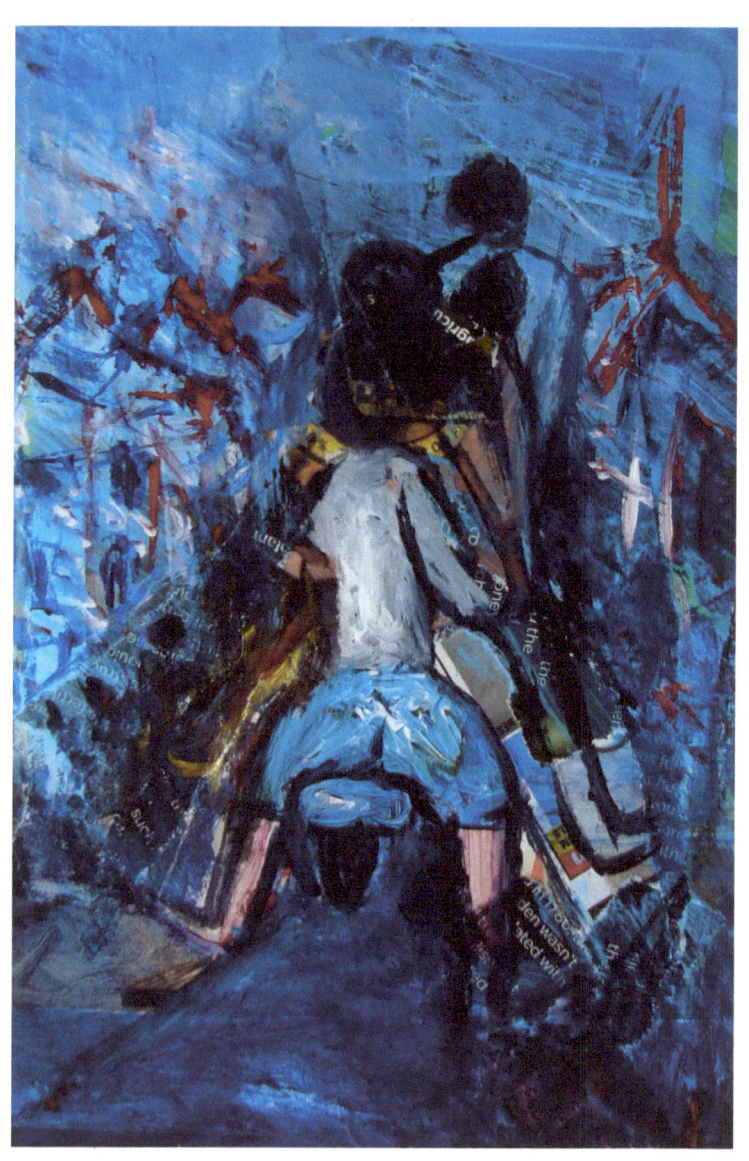

Home Sweet Home

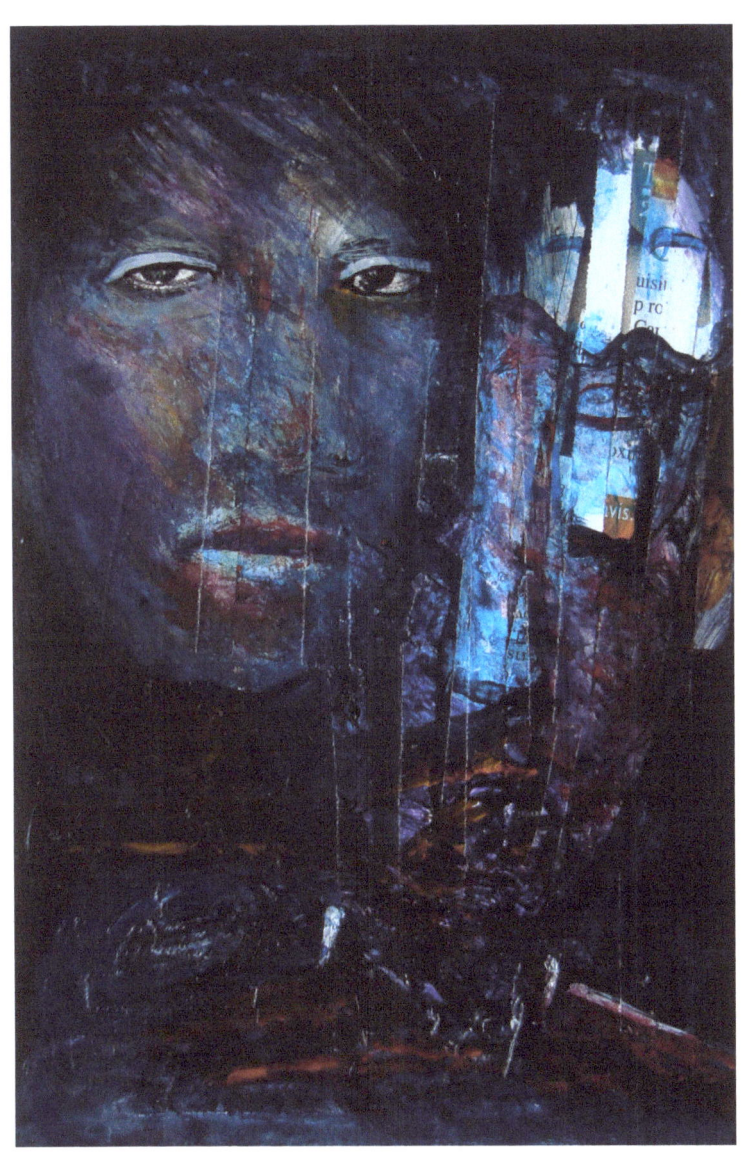

Kampuchea

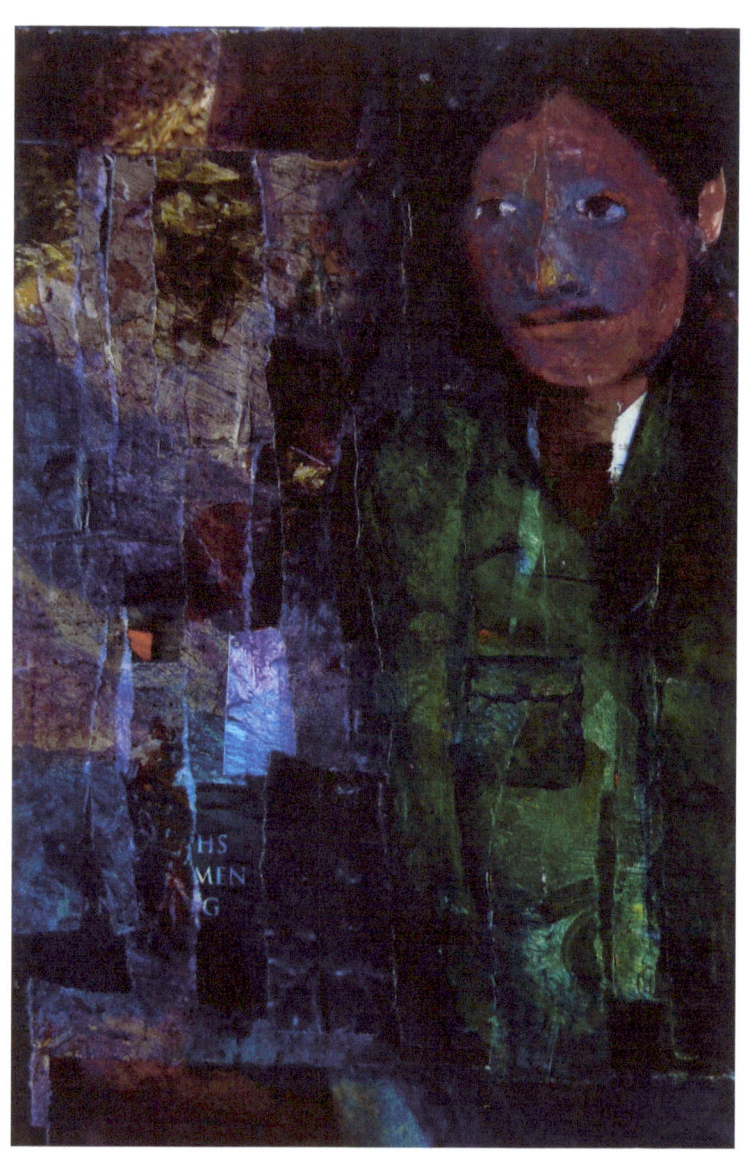

Stored in Pocket

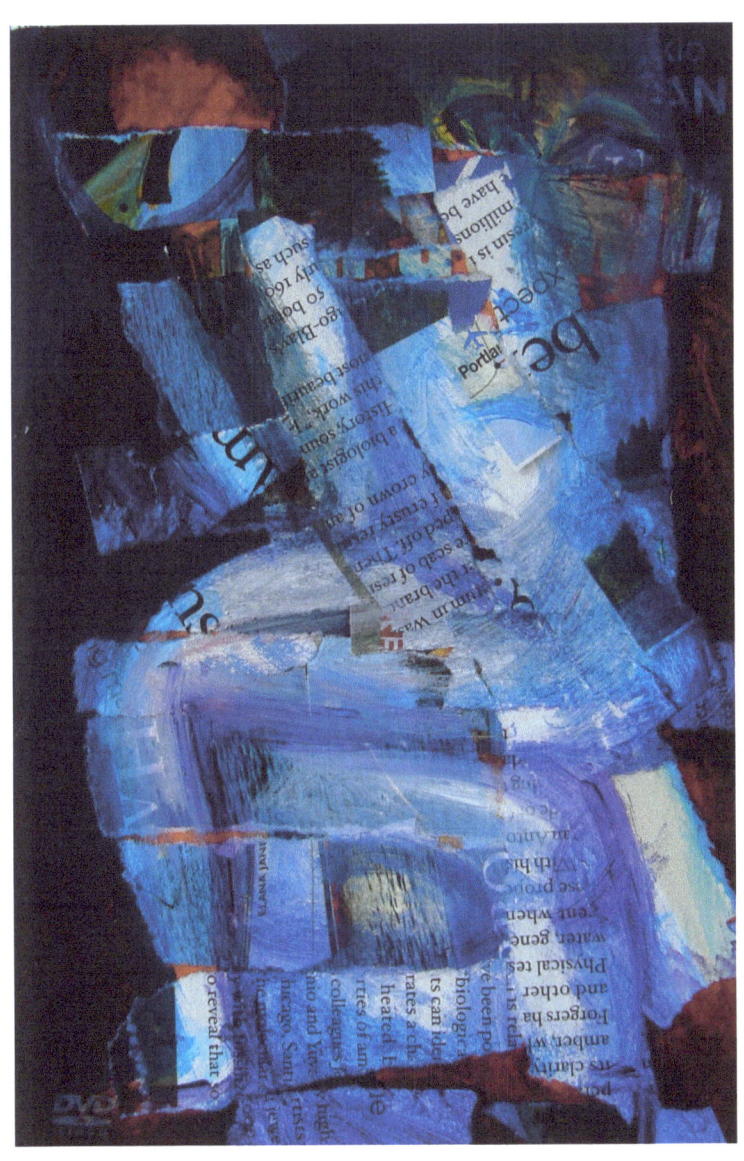

My Brother Thay

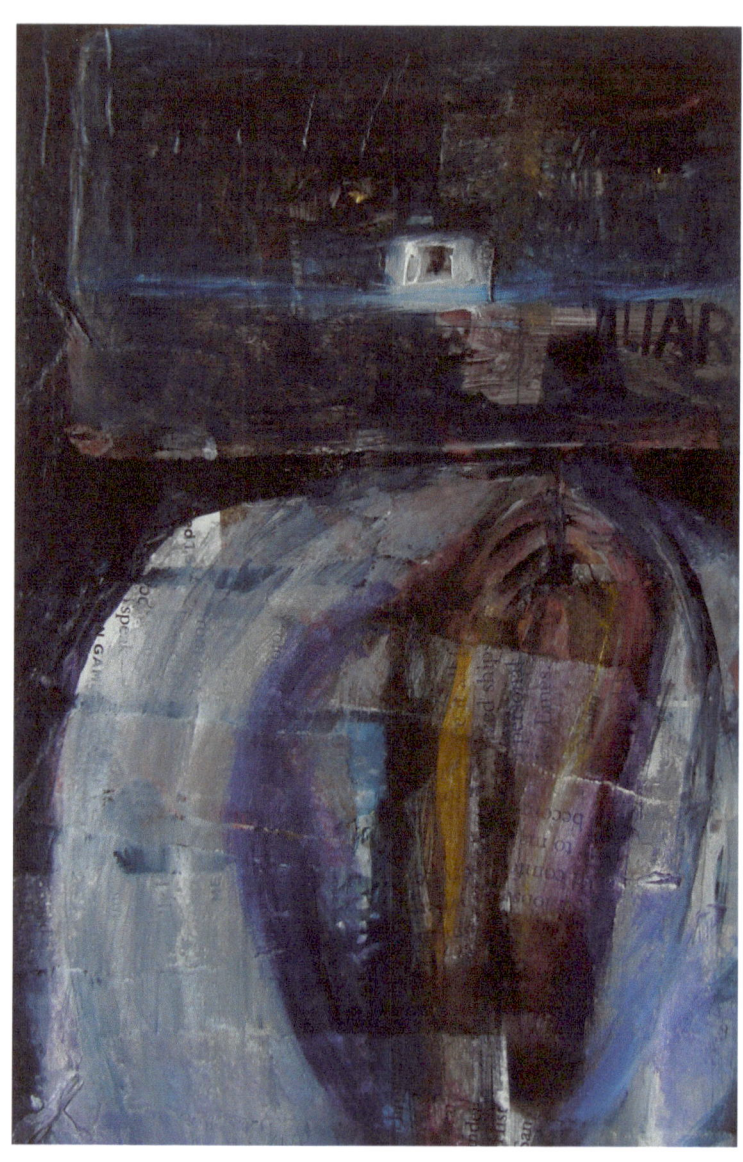

Briefcase Owner

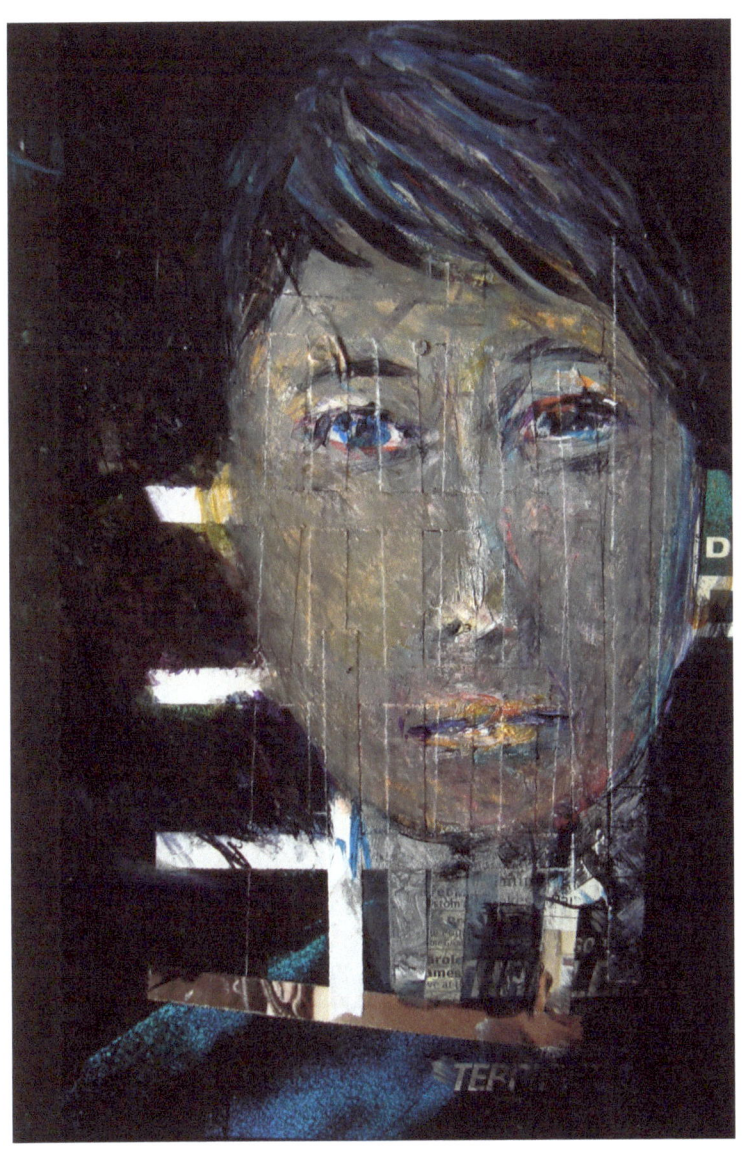

My House

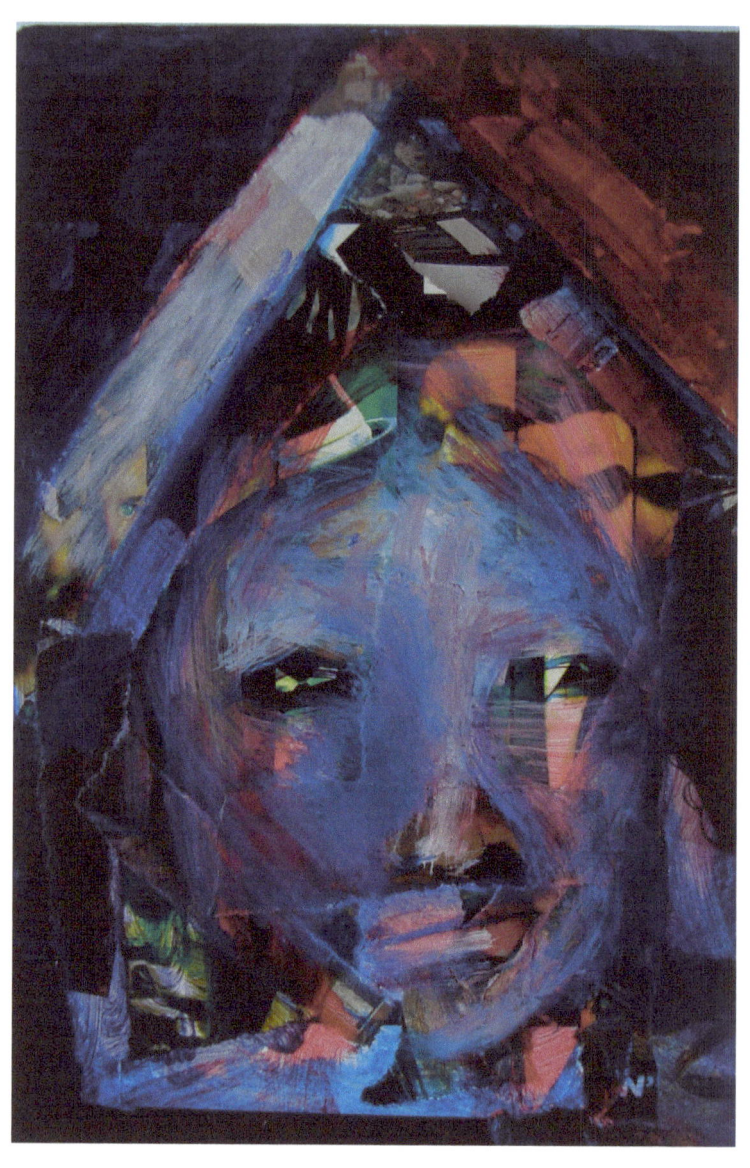

Roof Over the Heart

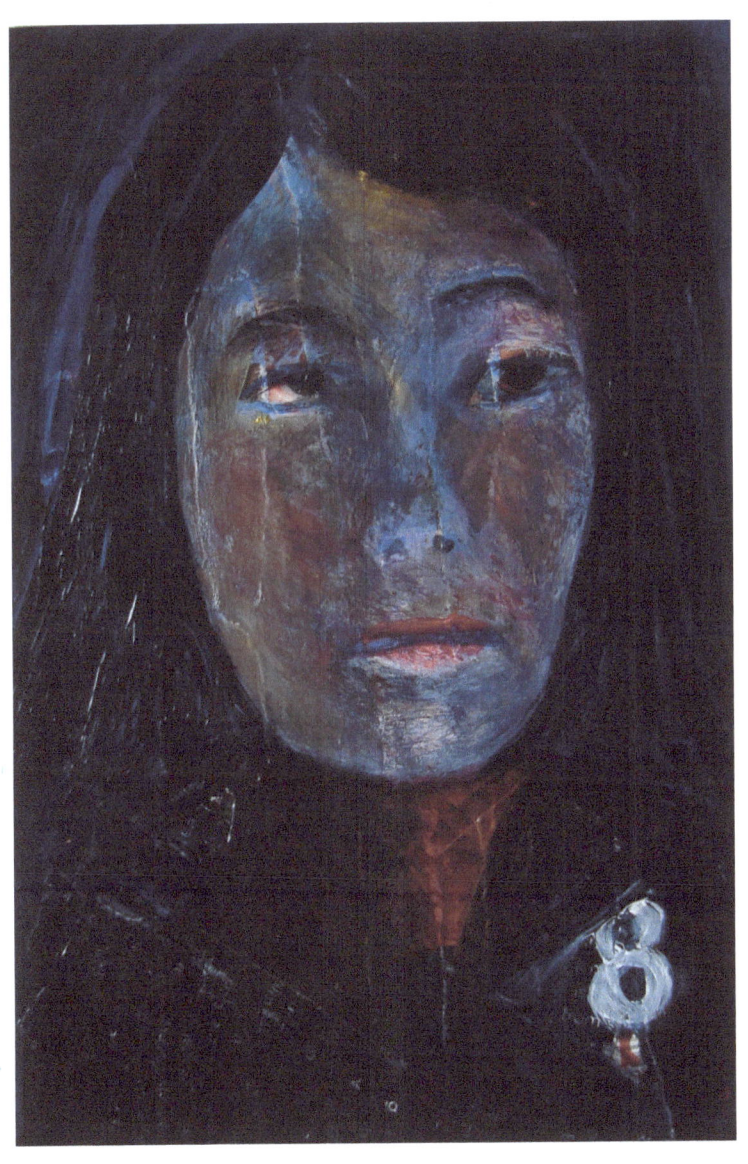

Number 8

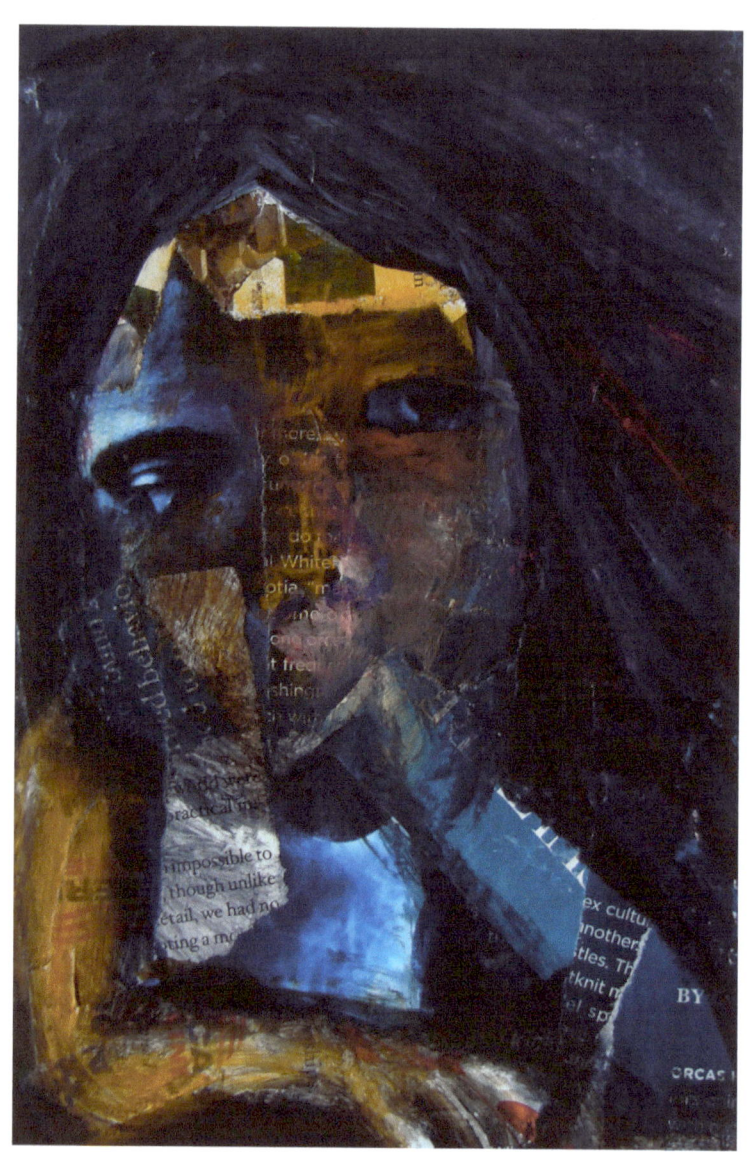

If Whores Were Witches

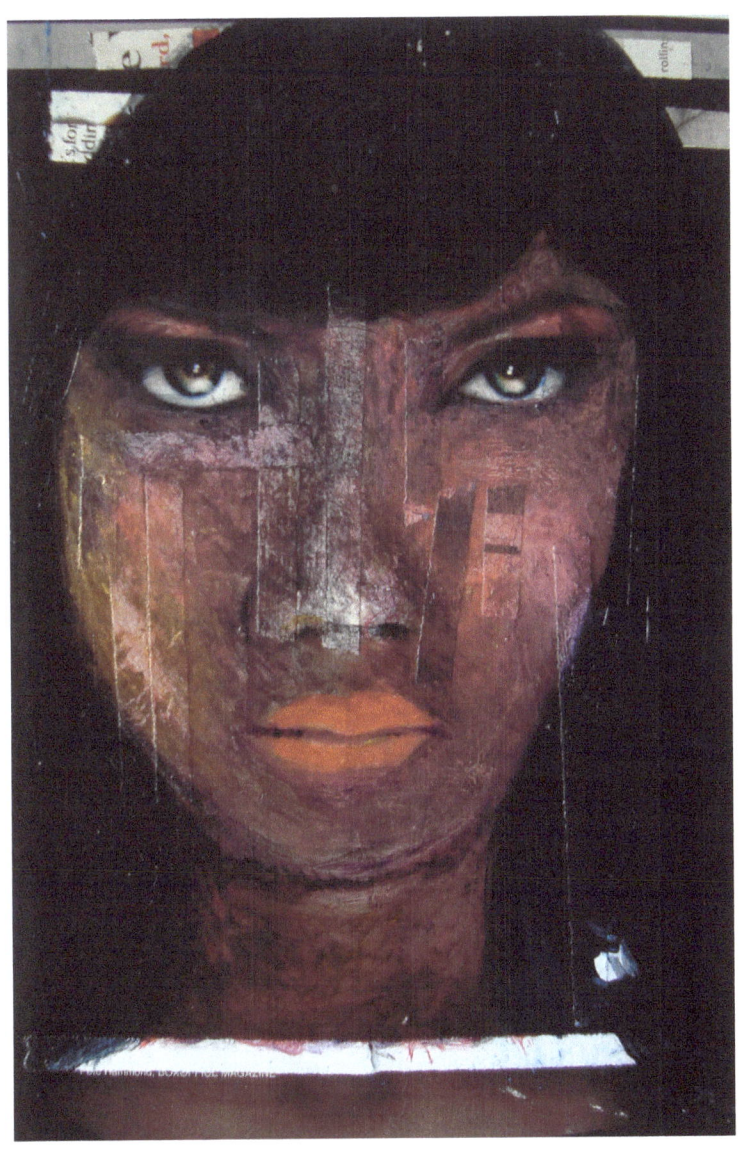

I Am a Karaoke Girl

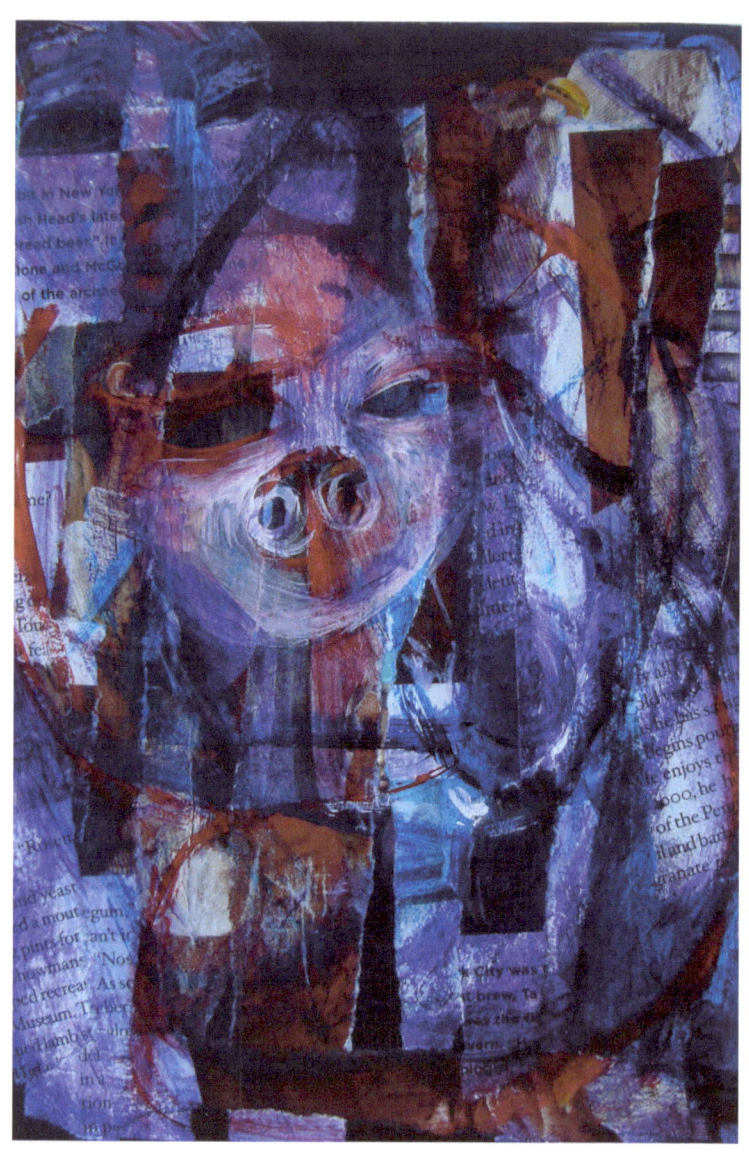

Karma...Maybe Next Life Better

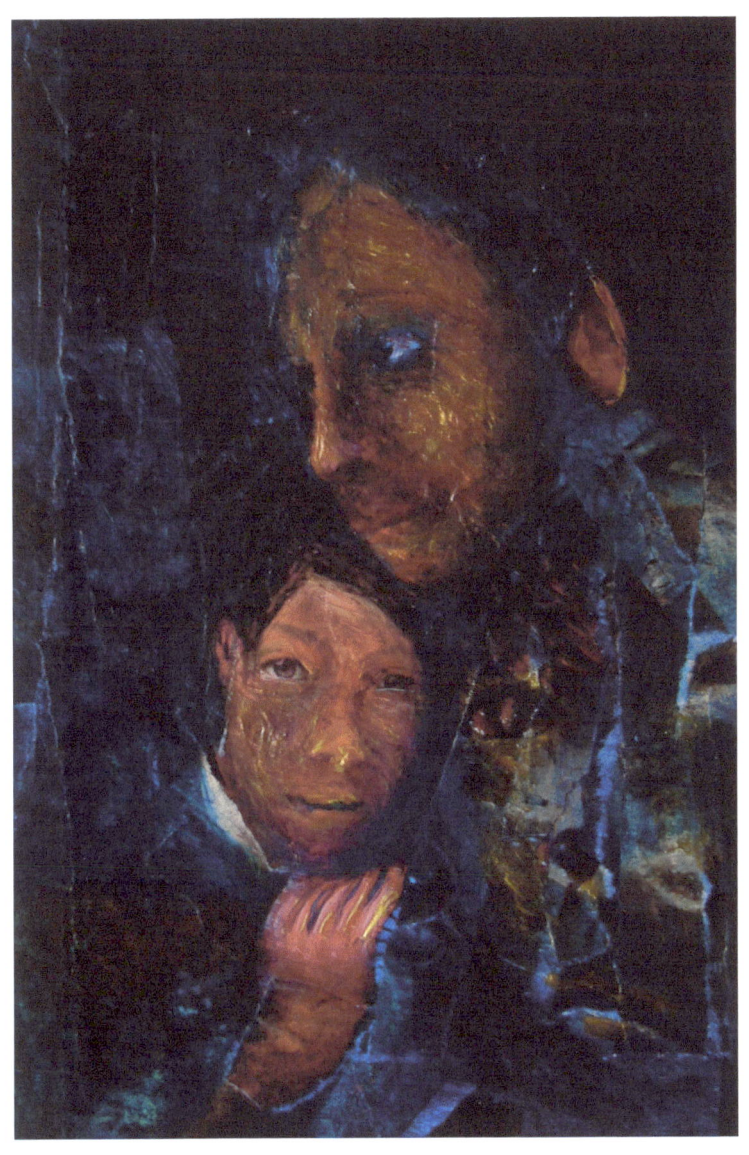

He's the One

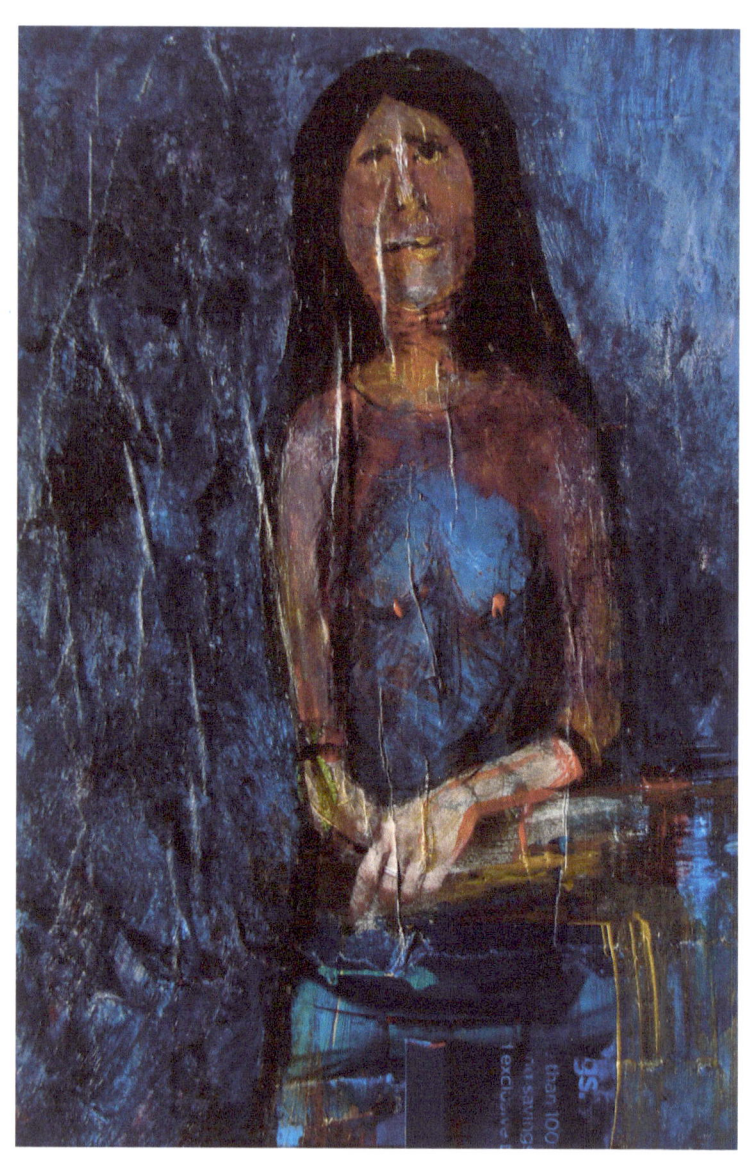

The Old Khmer Drag Queen

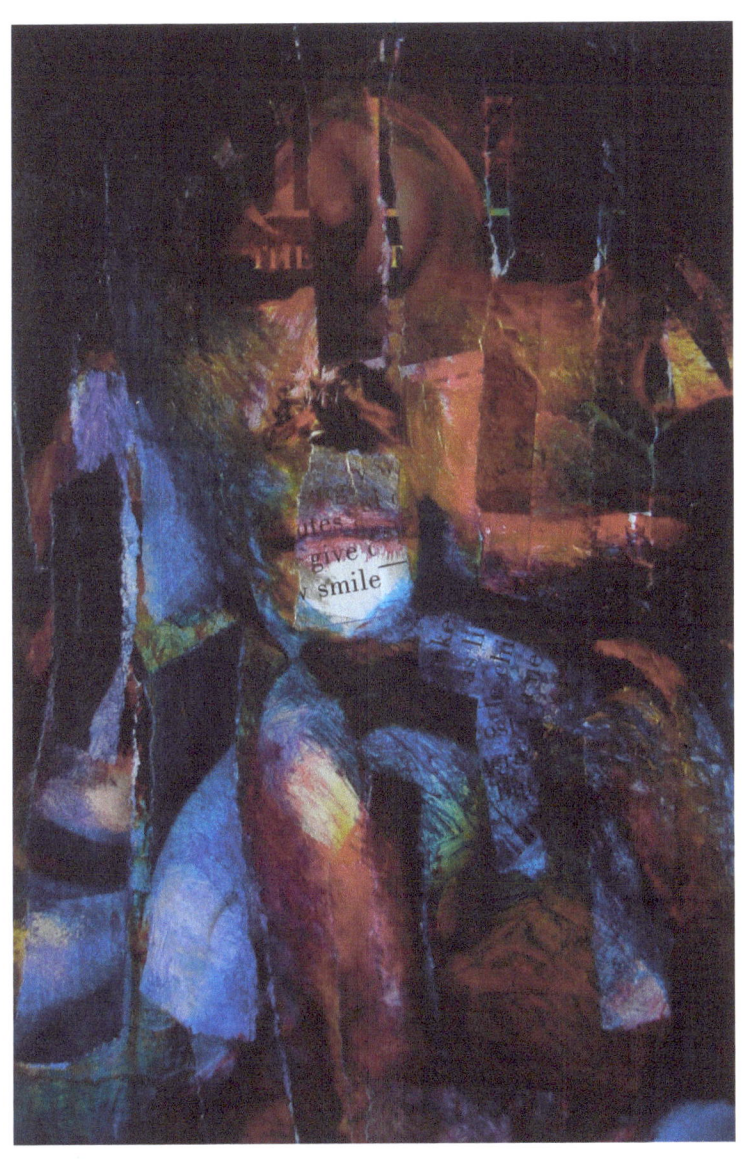

Love to a Man Who Loves Another Man

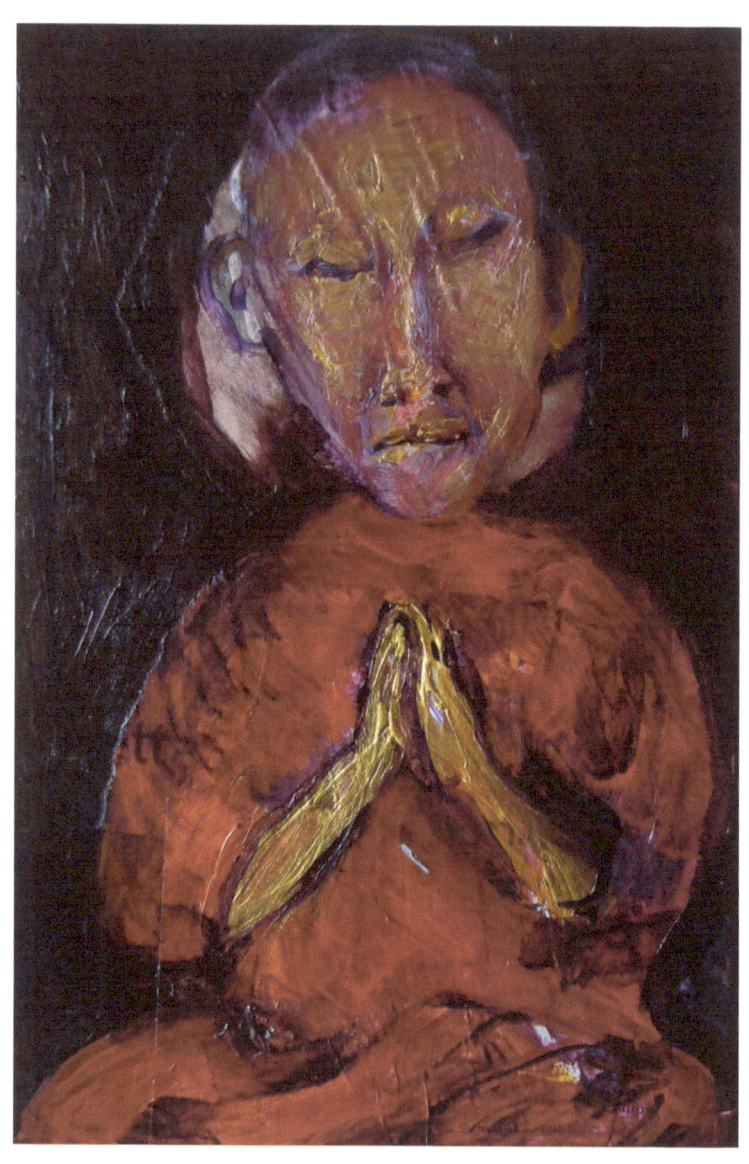

The Life of a Monk

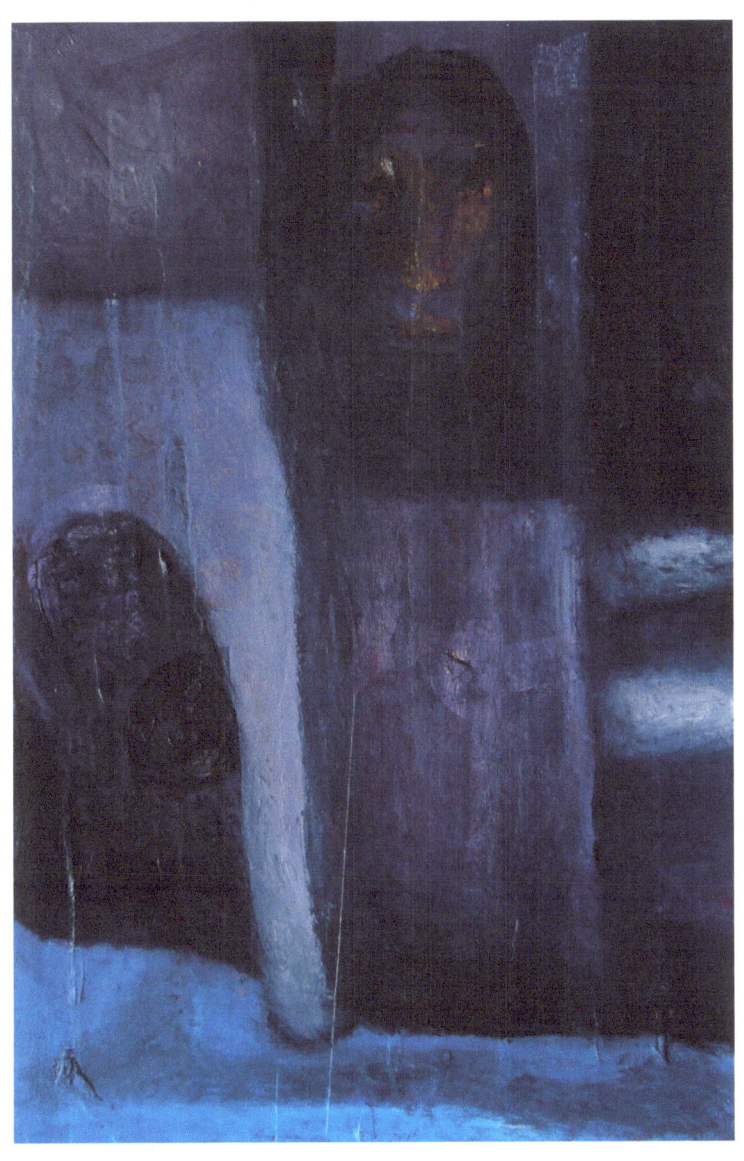

Misdiagnosed

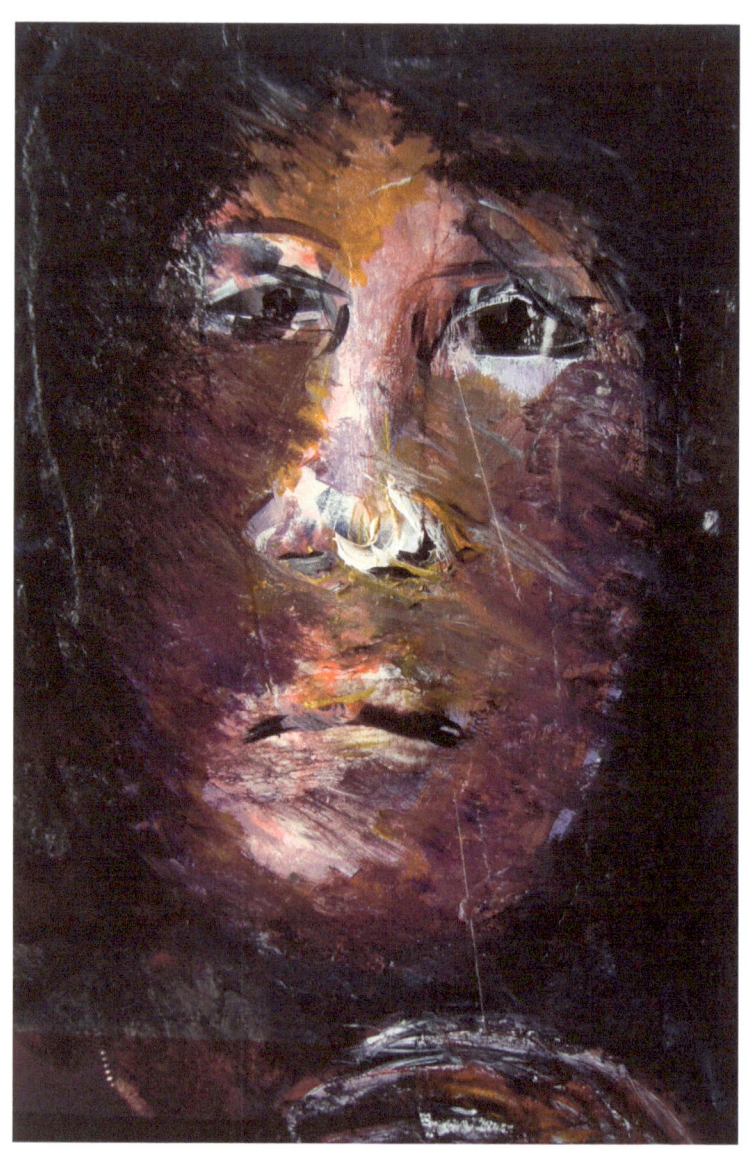

Ghost Monster

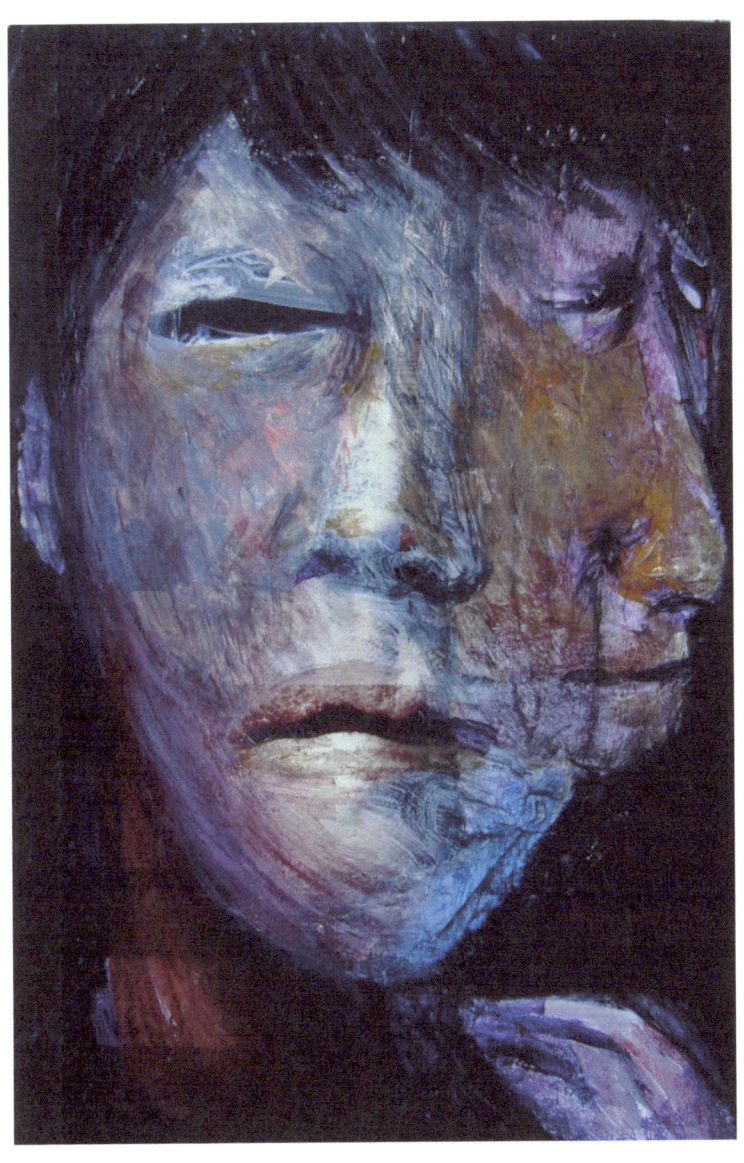

This Body Mystery

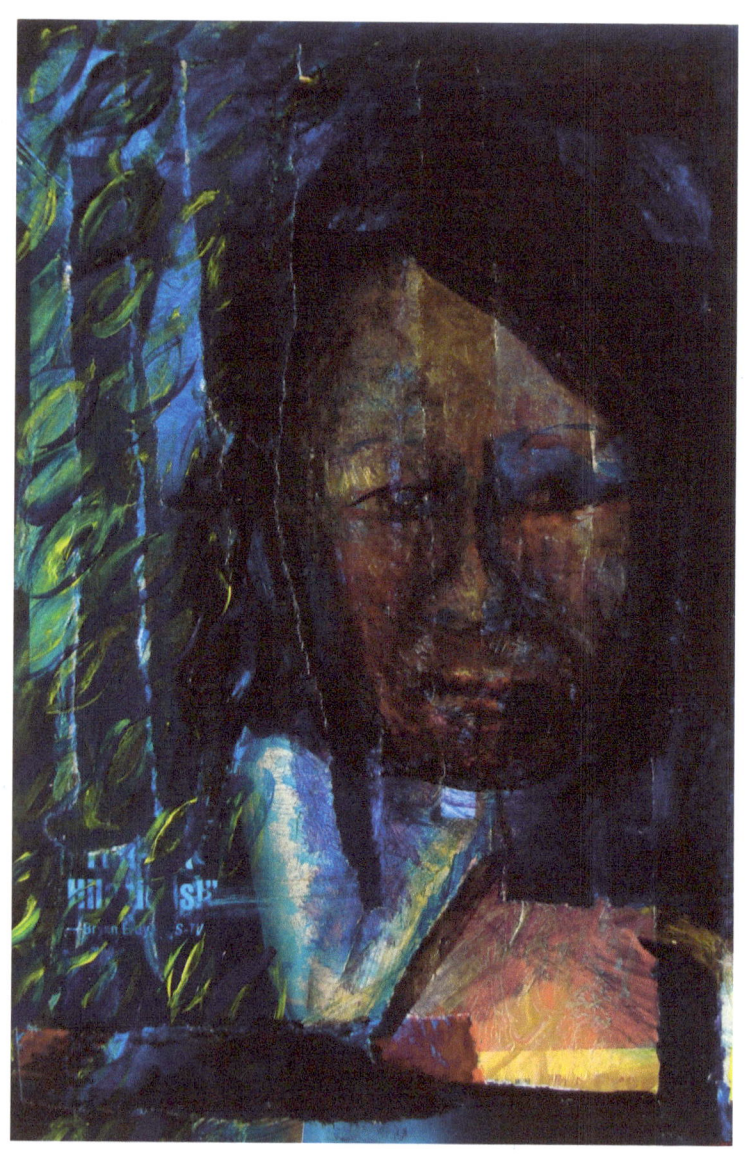

Bleakness...Dizziness

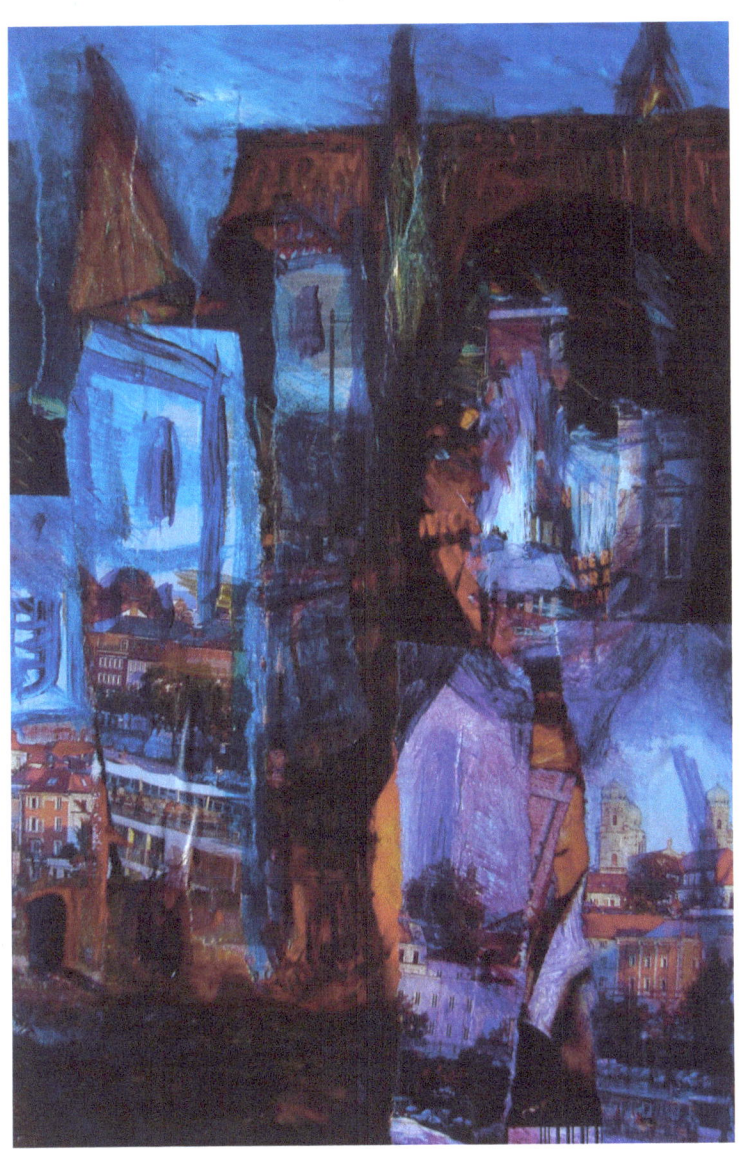

An Ode to Phnom Penh

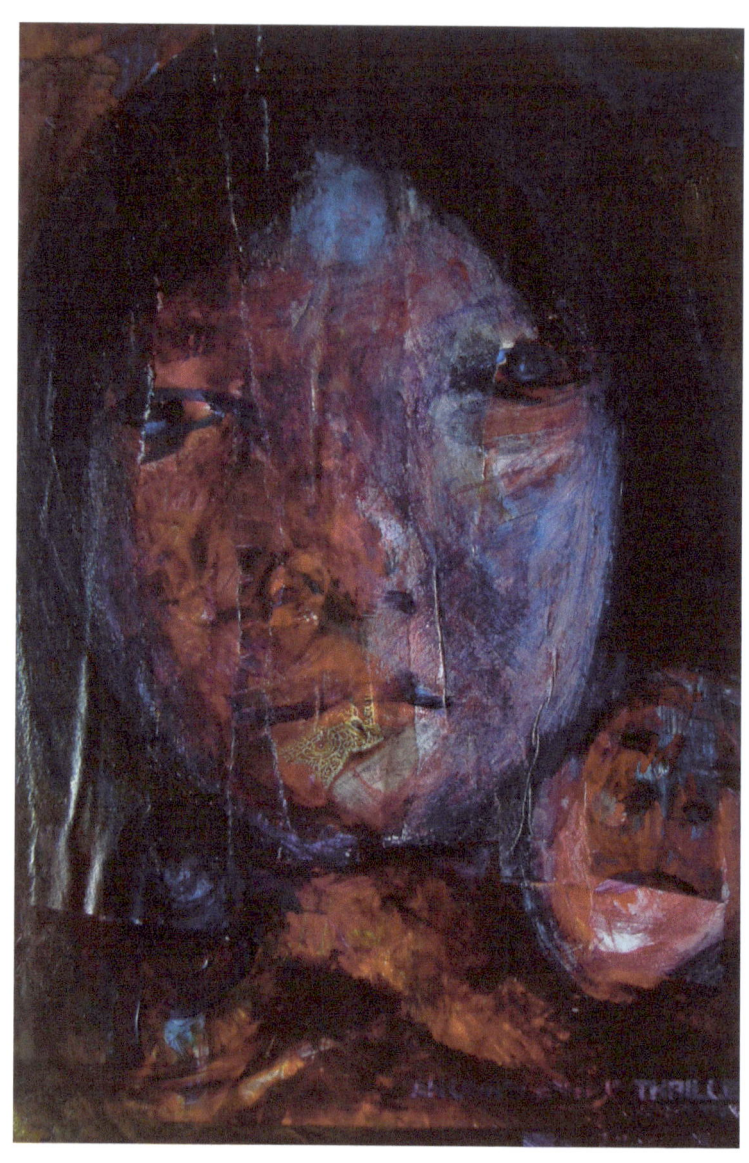

Exiting Interview

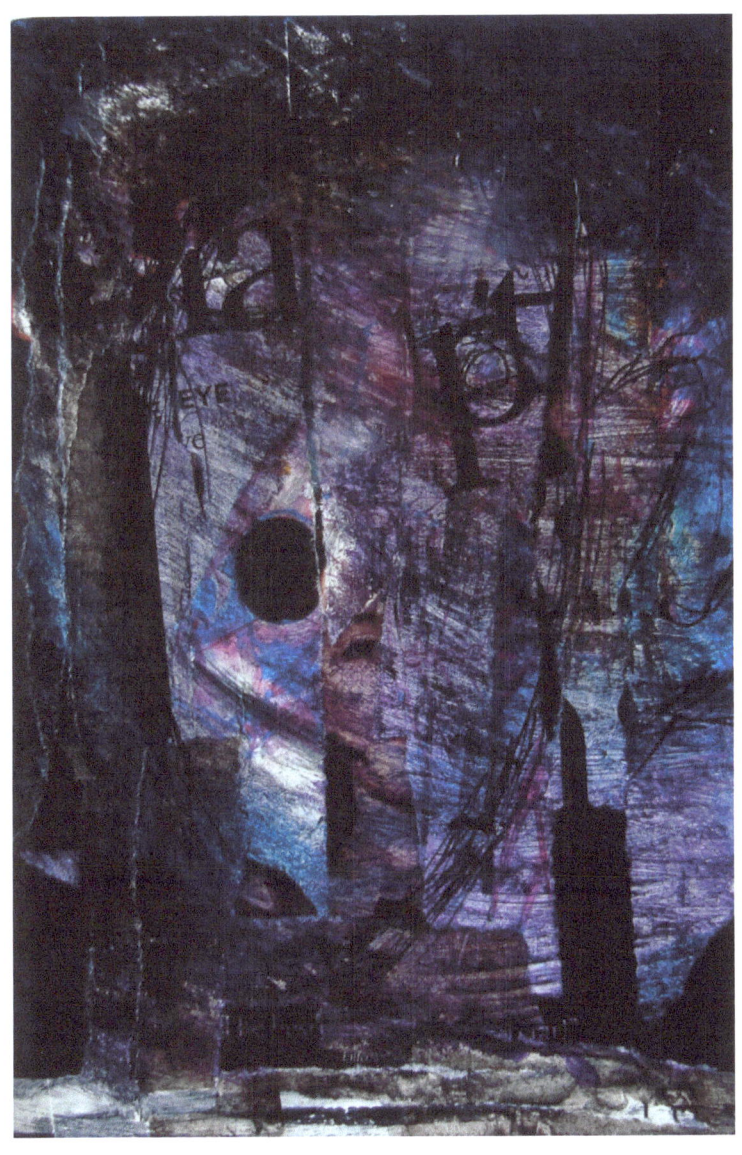

Death

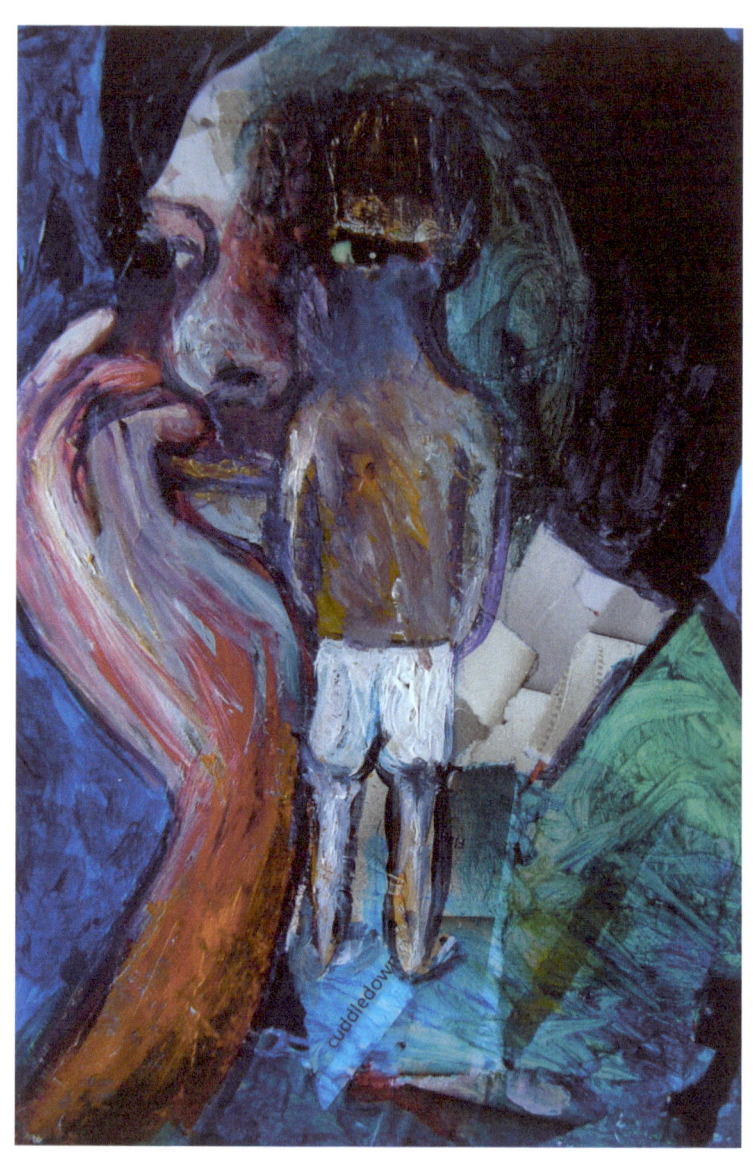

Swept Ashore Debris

this body
                    mystery

poems

Home Sweet Home

My life entrusted to strangers
Who drive moto
And wonder who I was,
Where I came from and why
I'm perched behind when
They should be driving
Wives and prostitutes to the movies.

My gated door shut, I'm alive to open it
Through dusted fumes, uniformed men
Mean familiar stares
And curious cats who tread
With confidence and arrogance.

They can shed more blood.
They will shed more blood.
They have shed more blood.

Acting out like cats in a clawing match
Answer-less questions hover
I arrive back at my gated door
And moto drivers leave taking their
Unfriendly manner, silence and private complaints.
I eat frozen, refrigerated rice from
Food sellers who advise me
"Buy everything fresh,"
"It's better."

Fresh or not, the cold rice tastes good hungry
I am the bourgeois and Envy
Even when I eat frozen food.

Kampuchea

The color of dark clay.
His face
His jaw bones knives,
His forehead skull
His head larger than his body.
His flesh a state of starvation

Stored in Pocket

Pictures of his wife and children –
A resume of a border camp
A diary to forget.

He jotted down the date
Of his interview with a US immigration officer.
Things he had to memorize to buy his way out of
miseries.
He lied.
Blame it on fate
His wife and four children immigrated.

He was alone,
A briefcase,
A bag of clothes
Fortunetellers saw only death in his future,
She lied to keep him hopeful.
Fought a guerrilla war
Frequented brothels.

Not even shrapnel
Could penetrate how
He lived. So what?

He fought for was disowned.
He had no rank.
He didn't know how to steal from others.
He crossed into Thailand as a common refugee.
He became another soldier in the family
To spend money on prostitutes
He learned to speak flawless, poetic Thai
To lure women into his bed.

My Brother Thay

That night he slept under guava trees
On a bamboo bed beneath a canopy of stars.
His older brother feared that he would infect his children
If he let him inside his thatched house.

He died with his eyes open
The virus spread its attack and pushed him with cold stiff feet.
It was silly to be monogamous.
There was no point to quit either drinking or smoking
That night he slept under guava trees.

Briefcase Owner

Combination lock
Regrets and memories
Buried over the years.

My House

high steps
door
my heart opens
shame and regrets;
blood it depletes

wounds enclosed
dark spots of my dark skin;
Lesions of HIV,
A foreign disease, a curse
karmic

Welcome to my house,
Thatched patches over my head,
Bamboo slats cushion my back,
The mat I use is woven red
From blind threads of human desire.

I need help
I am burning.
Put out the fire
I need a cure to swim in.
I want it bad.

Roof Over the Heart

A house that roofs over the heart

It is a place where roots can thrive
And branch out spreading from tree into shades
A home to return to when far

They scheme for more money, land, cars and houses.
A maid brings plenty of food
A home, he argues, is his private abode
His dreams and inspirations
Wings soaring

His life a larger purpose

bought wind sun and rain.

For I have earned what I have,
And when broken by despair

Mending begins
its power
Good or evil,
an instrument
the devil's only chance

And when my soul is in the right place,

life's purpose & dreams winged flights.

Number 8

I am number 8
squeezed tightly between sisters
behind a glass wall
numbered and tagged.

Chose me, I am the prettiest.
Just point me out to a bus boy.
He will come and get me.
I can be your Karaoke night, your dance girl,
your sex puff

Dance with me 'til you're sober.
Take me home when you're drunk.
Buy me! Whatever you pay
I keep half, half goes to my owner.

In my small provincial village,
there was no bar or nightclub,
no glittering neon lights, no dressing up for the party.
I had never worn high heels nor had a shiny blue gown.

As a little girl, I played grown-up with my friends
pretending we were actors and singers,
playing rich in our tattered clothes.
Mom and dad take us places in their nice big car.
We go to a fancy seafood restaurant,
and we eat Chinese noodles for breakfast.

Being a Karaoke star looked like so much fun
I play girl loves boy, boy loves girl
I sing and dance in the countryside with my nice
traditional Cambodian dress,

people powder me up to make me look pretty - lipstick,
rouge, eye shadow blue

I am a star, but I'm also a prostitute,
tricked and sold to a high class man
At first I was worth more than five hundred dollars
now, I can't even get ten dollars a night.

Some men are kind; others abusive and degrading
they look down on me because they pay for me
to perform sex.
When I don't feel like doing it I just close my eyes,
knowing tomorrow I'll face the mirror with tears
down my cheeks

I can never feel whole, marry and have a normal life,
unless a man whose love is so blind that he would
rescue me from the grip of poverty's
hand forcing me to prostitution
I am afraid. Once marked number 8
I will always be number 8.
Instead I want to end up an old, haggard woman
in the arms of someone I love.

If Whores Were Witches

The rice field – my playground
The Mekong – my swimming pool,
The water buffaloes – my companions.
My village
Time to plow
We plow,
Harvest we harvest

Men are idle in bar and brothel,
Whores were witches.
Scent of rubber mysteriously teasing the way sex stain had
Weaned my curiosity.
Sperm and rubber unveiled.
The heat of sex confirmed,
The need to touch cleared,
Understood.

I carry the memory of sex in the air,
Perverse scent slapping breasts and thighs.

I Am a Karaoke Girl

Straight black hair, fair complexion,
My round eyes a
Karaoke star,
 and man's duet in bed
And bar.

I sell beer.
Am beaten and raped
I light their cigarettes.
I wait on them.

I pour beer I play sexy I clean their trash.

I do anything.

Karma...Maybe Next Life Better

Your classy
Big air conditioning house
A land cruiser
Education
Sex
Buying love.

Me so cheap,
A peasant from the country,
I farm to feed and sell rice I can't buy to eat myself
My children head towards school
But lose themselves on dusty roads.

80% of Cambodia's poor
a short other extreme
I look for meals
You hoard food and stock
Make me desperate
You have choices
You take
My girls sold my boys somewhere on the street
gathering rubbish
Huffing
For money in the city
And with Aids
I have nothing to lose
My children gone fled
In city's brothels, bars and nightclubs,
Fending
Whoring
Dying young at the mercy of men
Who pay

Abuse them for sex

Karma. Maybe next life better.

My family name fades
My eyes falling
I am no one you know I never existed
Sun and darkness
Pain small, insignificant joy played out.

He's the One

Some nights my lover brings
Irises, chrysanthemum, lilies of the valley

Thumping
Secrets
Amass a mountain buried in snow

I'd let him come
Some uncertain distance
I'd undress for his kind, farmer's callous hands.

The Old Khmer Drag Queen

She stands in blackness adorned
By diamonds waiting for her man
Into the light, his love

Long black wigs flood her body
Her face a ghost strung on air
Waiting, curving, a red ant on two legs
In a tight black dress, vampiric
Her lover arrives, an appointment
With dark existence with day as an enemy.

The campy demeanor of her lover
With softened masculinity
Walks and swings his hands
Pushes his biceps and tightens his abs
To become a real man
The more he tries the greater
His breasts seem to grow
Sagging into formations only his
Western size bra can hold.

Love to a Man Who Loves Another Man

love to a man
who loves
another man?

Nights without days

Stars and moon the body digests

The heart clobbers and gulfs
Bites bitter sweetness stack
yearning
A monsoon orchestrated like
Fright
birds to dark tunnels.

His body a refuge
When possessed
he leaves.

it doesn't want a name

What it really wants is to be with just one man.

But what I must do I do so well
In spreading repose, my body
To break
 my heart a vessel
Never
I can,
I don't deny

a life

him

death

a raven's
squawking

he's never too cold.

The Life of a Monk

In a hospital bed
Flat spring no mattress,
Dust stained walls enclosing my face
Geckos haunting death to take us.

My body light and drugged
Set afloat
Clouds
Leaving dawn to its nest
My fingers absent of feelings, my toes detached
cartilages,
Arms and legs in separation, taking my pieced and
sewn soul.

My life, as I know it, is fleeing from my lungs,
My heart a distant chanting of monks
Lost to celibacy
My passion.

A celibate promise to nirvana,
Suppressing
Nurtured
To feel because I am human.

A mortal path to grace, trial and error.

Misdiagnosed

My brother went from one traditional healer to another.
Each healer prescribed a different cure
That made his condition worse.
Hopeless
Night fevers and sweats.
Esophagus with lesions.
We brought monks to chant for him.
Paid the village doctor to give him IV injections of glucose.
Nothing worked.
He became gaunt
His knee caps, his skull
His large eyes sockets.
A casket was brought in.
His body washed and dressed.
The monks returned to chant.
A picture of Buddha with his bright, flickering halo
Hung before the wooden casket.
That night the children stayed up to watch Karaoke.
Chicken and fish rice porridge
Before the funeral procession
Laid in a ditch the size of his body.
The smot death music I hear floating out
Takes me.

Ghost Monster

A ghost, a monster in my dream.

Every night, the scent of another woman,
the foul mix of brothel and alcohol.
He stays behind
cruel and distant.

His life is secret
I continue to spread out for him,
Every time he crawls up my spine.

This Body Mystery

a shell, a borrowed ship, a vessel leaving.
I want this body to go
And take this virus with it.

Bleakness...Dizziness

There's weight   there's lightness
I feel light   I can almost fly run after
Falling leaves swept by the wind

An Ode to Phnom Penh

arrive
From you
I depart

Birth and childhood you I remember palace
and pagodas in seamless stream
Old and new you remake yourself the envy of every city in the
world
Had worn down to squalid Your foul smell, your love scent of a
different era
Your genocide museum darkness hovering over me Your
government rodents squandering the night Your rich men's
bellies protruding Taking slowly the blood and sweats of the
poor streets and large boulevards French and colonial
Your traffic blood on asphalt Your cyclos and motodops
nostalgia loosing its breath
Oh, how you sing badly in karaoke bar and nightclubs Your
voices of social judgment and class disturbances inhuman acts
bleeding peace morning and night you sing and life you live
Sounds of construction and roaring traffic
Yet I love you skin hugging bone
You are beautiful again from death you are reborn a thousand
times stronger
Sniffing your foul air as palm sweet
From the countryside
Your Mekong and Tonle Sap converse

Secrets of joy the world would die for,
If only your hiding smile on a lotus bloom can only be theirs
Bought and sold, for your pride and dignity are made of gold.

Exiting Interview

Do you remember the month or the exact day of your
birth?

Have you been anywhere outside your village?
Do you have properties in your name?
Do you want to go now or do you want to stay?
How many children are you leaving?
Do you have any other relatives who will care for them
when you're gone?
How old are your children?
What inheritance are you leaving for them?
Is this your thatched roof house?
How about these pots and pans?
Do you own land?
Are these your regrets?
How often have you known grief and sorrow?
Who mistreated you?
How did you arrive in poverty?
How did you come to loneliness?
Did you have a first love?
Was the marriage what you expected?
Was it an arranged marriage?
Who was your husband?
Do you know him?
Do you have AIDS?

Death

I'm going to spit in your face.
Don't wink and flirt with me.
I am not interested.

Claim someone else.
I am not ready!
I am not dying for you.

Swept Ashore Debris

On low tide sand, where uprooted trees
Resemble birds and man,
Wings widespread torsos half buried
In shallow water
We collected broken
Bottles, China and jars salt cut into forms

sun darkened my dark skin

James, bare
white burned red tan
scouting sea treasure
became a dot, a capsized view
In my wandering, distant eyes

Oh, how I wanted to love him
But I didn't want him to run
a shore not his
Bolton farm where Ken's arms
Love me
he'd love me.

other poems

The Road Home

Road
home
— past life and garbage
Feces I cleaned
inside

tattered heart.
I tasted my country's bitter roots,
And I wanted to run as far as I could,
stay among lingering, infesting
Wounds so flies have a reason to live.
Still unsatisfied
I am ready death.

The Refugee

I belong here, I think,
Though the rain blood in my eyes
A picture too cruel
I can't remember far

Too close my heart rejects
I am driving somewhere to forget
Of highways only I can't describe
A tunnel of air fill my lungs
My driver's side shield down
I think of a place I can't return

A father gone by the bullet of war
a history tragic smeared and blood
murders the world ignored
the loneliness I now feel even among
civilized people
cold and withdrawn
my life silent
tongues shot mute
as if the ocean
is being sucked away into space
leaving us to burn blacker

I vomit at the thought of another war

Lowell Life

Lowell grim
A hurry crying traffic
Honking impatiently
Potholes
Dollars
Just to pay insurance companies
For sickness

For the car I drive
Roof over my head
For the telephone no one calls
For the television I don't watch
For the internet I hide in
For the company of strangers
Murderers
I bring home
Every client
Thirty one dollars
Afloat
On the American dream
Better to die happy
Then sad

Lots of possessions

An American life is not working.

A Foreigner in My Own Country (Barang)

God &
forsaken country

Children with scraggly, sun bleached hair
The color of metallic rust
Shirtless
tattered shorts
Are chasing after oxen and water buffalo
In parched, impoverished blood drenched rice field
I once had roamed

charred by bombs.

Displaced and uprooted
My dream

blue skies absent of birds

La Voyage

In a crowded plane
I sit wondering what if the plane crashes
And I am forced to embrace this stranger next to me
Who doesn't talk nor does he want to shake my hand
I can't ask his name
Because I don't speak his language,
But I like looking at him when he sleeps
His eyelids pink a little skin rouge
The color of a baby mouse
Its skin a touch of glow as it breathes
Its eyes shut as it searches for milk severing its hunger.
His brows bend toward the shape of his forehead.
His hair curls blond.
His nostrils dark tunnels full of clogged air
His snore a little lion chasing its prey
I wish I can touch his legs
Or finger comb his hair
I wish I can kiss his eyes
And look into his glass covered vision to see what's there.
I want those lips open so I can give him all my air
The plane can crash anytime
I wouldn't care as long as I can embrace this man
With the plane no longer there.

La Voyage 11

In a half empty plane
The window seat
a view to a dead stillness
Of overcast clouds
the tarmac
a Chinese barks

Demanding I get up for his seat
When I got the right place right pass

And the two men sat down
With their unfriendly stare

Looking over me head to toes
Uncultured and unmannered

When all I wanted was to be left alone
A seat to myself with an empty air space
To close my eyes in peace
I imagine the plane plunging

From the Womb

From the womb tyranny!
"A blue, gravitational ball"

From the womb tyranny
A place once warm cold
Kind…cruel
Drowned down in children's blood
And salt from their dead eyes
Poisoning the rice fields.

Demons and black kings
In guards
Stood ruins
Gripped by uprooted trees
In mass graves
A voice slit shut
Fractured into arms

One tyrant inherited
Crowds of greed
To burn down their
Own villages shouting
Rouge a foreign word
Their songs Chinese in translation
Mao the slanted jade
An allure
To hate foreigners
And local puppets
And their white fingers
Playing Chopin.

Language kept the peasants chained.
(dark savages in their own house)
colonized
Trashy whites
From every breed

Owned disowned
Their science power
Superstitious and black
Untouched (and every bomb dropped)
On the miseries of those they seek
How dark their hearts
How flat the earth
A blue, gravitational ball.

Rouge

Kill one kill
all
they say
Leave no blood line
for revenge

Trembling,
Tears down his cheeks
A man,
His father's age,
In black like a raven.

His face light in the dark, glowing
His eyes cat hazel marble clear!

His fingers long, slender and fragile
Takes out his spleen
He commands!
The grill is ready.

The boy died with hiccups.
His head is on the ground.
His heart wound down

I am powerful said the man.
I have demonic power.
I am rouge.

Bamboo Bush/Kapok Tree

Returning,
Sixteen years of smells and sounds
A Cambodia/Campuchea of a different time
No, neither guns nor exploding bombs.

They tell me
Phnom Penh is full of people.
I've forgotten, I've read of emptiness
Weddings and deaths.
They tell me
I could never understand the destruction wrought

They tell me

I left
On foot,
Hunted in Thailand on to America
We were all fleeing, making safety and fame, for war
and genocide.

Nothing is familiar
About my home – the river drove on
The Kapok tree my mother had planted.
My sister had told me to look for a bush of bamboo
But they are everywhere and how could she remember
If I couldn't – I asked an old man Grandfather if he
Knew my sister Sareen and shaking he didn't know my
Father Uy Lam. But everyone knows him and I am
His youngest son but fingers point north further on
Toward woman squatting under a Kapok Tree not
asking

Questions about mangoes or bamboo.
The missing fence and house not embraceable but my
mother's
Voice echoes back, telegraphed limping home from the
market
Past a broken bridge where a machine gun was
searching
For an idyllic view.
No house. No pond. No bamboo.
No lemon grass.

Taking Her Place Behind Some Bushes

Trembling a witness
Your husband and children
Imploring them
To save from a distance in silence
Buddha
When they screamed
You wanted them to live
You wanted them to die quickly.
With quick bullets
Don't torture them
Don't beat them.
Don't laugh at them.
Don't drain their blood.
Don't see anymore.
Don't take out their eyes.
Don't eat their livers even if you want.

Behind those bushes
Where she left her life.
Her eyes, her memories.

Dead Girl in a Muddy Pond

First they circle
Spit curses
Your face a laugh
A fear

They want your body sister.

They want your womb.

The young wife of their enemies
Virgin breasts for their fun
They can drag and pin you down
Your springtime floating
In a muddy pond.

In a field of water
Floating, a cradle
Of arms nobody can tell you otherwise.

Those Hateful Beasts

In Long Beach
A Cambodian sits by the window
The Khmer Rouge scars
Of her violations
Where neither birds nor blue sky.

She stares sharply
She is still there
And children and apartment
Covered with Graffiti share spaces with
Pests, a man's thumb sits pondering the blood
Her husband was dragged bayonets poking
A chain of humans
Her sons like marching skeletons
Robbed of their clothes into annihilation
And shoved
Chambered
Dismembered
For amusement.

The Khmer Rouge took a palm leaf
And setting it like a razor
Sliced away
Children and skin and drained blood
In a bowl with slain chickens.

My Mother's Best Friend

Ama-rich,
Where wealthy people live,
Giant houses, with money
Explaining poverty
The humid
Dust smothering village
Missing the monsoon
Cacophony of dirt roads cutting

No phone
Electricity
A kerosene lamp
A car battery to light your house
I told her
CHANGING, she tells me
Your mother was alive

Go to the casino in Poipet
Chinese soap operas
Chickens
Patch of vegetables
The rain falls less and less
Poor people
Ama-rich

In factories under the table
Friend's relatives say
That in Ama-rich
No matter how poor
You can survive
The poorest in Ama-rich

Still drive a Mercedez
She raises her thumb.
Eyes like my mom's black
Clear and teary, smiling shining black teeth
Chewing betel nuts and tobacco

In Ama-rich.
Waiting to die.

Absence

Born of absence
In a jaw of salt pickled eggs
I hatched without a tongue
And a sight feathers grew black too short to fly.

My wings absent of dreams
There's no road from the rice fields
Too blind to have clawed
I am invisible, I am absence.

Mistress

a villa
maids
A chauffeur
my Lexus
he can take

be my rose
And my doll
You won't have to worry
When I am lonely, it's you I want to see

cell phones
a heart beat
close to your ear
You'll hear me say, hello, my darling

So I believed him
Until one day, his jealous wife
Threw a jug of acid at my face

I scream melting for his name
But the old man
ran away

Low High Tides

High tides life low
Low tides life high

Give me the salt oh waves
Crash into my heart
Give me the fins of sharks
Impale me with your sea urchins

Roar from the abyss of your ocean's bed
And vomit ashore
madness
Wash down this life's uncertainty
And take what remains of my existence

In your cradle rock me in your net
Hook me 'til I bleed
Never again will I taste
This earthly salt of hate.

Creator Destroyer

What in turn becomes acts of evil.

Once, I had wanted to be Shiva,
With many arms
and the power
To create/
destroy the world.

Used to beguile evil with justice,
And when forced to bleed
My power creator destroyer
Weapons
Become
Acts
Of evil.

Fatherland

a rapist in sarong,
My fatherland his foreign penis
in sagging position,
Smoking Marlboro light like a homeless
Dog, vile and scraggly
While another man and his conquistadors
Wear dollars over their eyes commanding existence.

Their wives and mistresses, in their leisure hours,
At war, acid throwing, and disfiguring beautiful, lightened
white skin virgins.

Men of power,
Behind their skirts,
would make the animal kingdom
Looks like a democrat
'Cause they can only bark out their own importance.
Every bag of rice, a bottle of soy sauce
A bundle of incense sticks to the villagers to threaten for
their votes.
To their dark skinned driver's birth place,
Where villagers, old and young, squat with mouths agape

In the scourging sun
Their hands clasped subservient

If I Had a Country

If I had a country would I be so lonely?

If I had a house would I stay to tend a rose garden?

In changeable arms of lovers who would take
What they need and leave me empty?

If I had private wings of a metal bird
Where would I go?

Phnom Penh, in foreign bars drinking bought beer
By white men who think Asians are exotic?

Boston,
With a bouquet of flowers he gathered from his field?

If I had myself would I be a vagabond whoring
The world in search of love among these men
Whose love I don't feel?
Or will I stay put to tend the fields I once
Knew?

Shortcomings

Neon lights stripes of streets
Many colors exposed where stripes of darkness
Lines black and white shades of gray
Day the sun
Night electric
Work and no play for some money in many bank accounts
Walls Street
Investment
Index pages of high and low
Interest rates, bond a bondage
Of sex and industrialized human miseries
Globalizing human trafficking of women
And children into bars and nightclubs
Appearing from artificial heavenly clouds
Angel faces vaginas and penises up for sale stripe and poll
dancing
Like chimpanzees from tree to tree
Techno music sound of machines
Becoming human inhabiting feelings
Legs thighs in sweating coils
Eyes divine mirrors of the soul
Purple haze and drugged
Cigarettes and alcohol
Marijuana on tongue a kiss of death
Take home an increase in pay

The weaker man the women and children

Index of Color Plates

All paintings are collage and acrylic on movie postcards,
5.5 x 8 inches, 2011